AF350596

Different Tales
(A Children's Book)
By Rea-Silvia Costin, P.E.

Print ISBN: 979-8-3306-7215-8
EBOOK ISBN: 979-8-3306-7216-5

This book is dedicated to my beloved brother Costin, Radu Apostol
and to the wonderful childhood memories we shared together.

Table of Contents

... about me

published my first book *Short Stories: The Story of a Refugee* with Vantage Press in 1997 and republished it independently in 2023. In 2003, I published the first book of a trilogy, *Thiana-AVDELA-A Macedonian Village in the Northwestern Greece: Thiana's Native Land* and in 2004 and republished it independently in 2024; I published the second volume of the trilogy *ATHENS* with iUniverse and republished it independently in 2024. American Publishing Company has published the third book of the trilogy, *America-The Final Destination* in 2006 and republished it independently in 2021.

American Publishing Company also published my first poetry book, *Pearls on a String: Love Songs Volume I,* in 2006, then republished it in 2020 with Author's Press.

My poetry is published in *The Best Poems and Poets of 2001, 2002, 2003,* and *2005, The Theatre of the Mind,* and *The Celebrations of Honors* as well as *Who's Who in Poetry 2004, 2005, and 2007* editions by the International Library of Poetry. In May, 2002, I obtained my Laureate Certificate from the International Library of Poets. I am the recipient of the Editor's Choice Award, 2002, 2003, 2005, and 2007 from the poetry.com site as well as the President's Award for Excellence in Literature from the National Authors Registry.

In January 2005, I joined the Poets.com Workshop under the pen name of Frantzi500 (my nickname).

My second poetry book *Pearls on a String: Love Songs- Volume Two* was published by Publish America in 2009 and republished it in 2020 with Author's Press.

In this book, *Different Tales: A Children's Book*, I selected few stories (some of them part of my previous published books) that I thought would be enjoyed by a younger audience. The stories are arranged in a somewhat chronological sequence, following my life's experiences, back in Romania, then in Greece, and now here, in the U.S.A. The tales also refer to my profession as an engineer and my faith as a Christian.

Women in Religion

I was thinking of the role women had in the history of mankind, and thought about writing about how women are depicted in the Bible.

We all remember the Book of Genesis, and how God created the earth, and separated the earth from the waters, and created the sky and the stars, and the night and the day, and brought light to Earth, and created the trees and the grass.

Then God created the animals that inhabit the earth, and the fowl that inhabit the sky, and the fish that inhabit the oceans, and put man in charge of them.

And all the animals had their own mates: Mr. Bear had Mrs. Bear, Mr. Rabbit had Mrs. Rabbit, and Mr. Lion had a Mrs. Lion, but Adam was alone.

God saw that Adam didn't have a mate and thought that was not good!

So God created Adam's mate from Adam's rib while he was asleep, and named her Eve; he gave her to Adam to be his helper.

So, you can see that while God created Adam from dust, Eve was created from Adam's rib as an extension of Adam's body, or part of the same body.

What is the real meaning of this? In the same what that the word woman adds the prefix "wo" to the word man, a woman's place is to serve her man.

Is this a good thing? or bad?

It depends on whom you are asking.

If you ask some men they will respond: "Yes, it is good!"

If you ask a woman, especially a liberated woman, the answer is: "Nonsense! We can live without men and be happier!"

About 10-15 years ago, to make up for my lack of education in the Bible, I started to read it from page 1 to page 1,731. The project took me about 3 years, because I could not read more than 10 pages before I fell asleep.

So, let's take a look at women depicted in the Bible, and try to figure out their role and contribution to mankind.

Who does not remember the story of beautiful Sarah, which means "woman of high rank," and her husband, Abraham, the father of nations? Sarah gave birth to Isaac at the age of 90 years old and he started the nation of Israel. Meanwhile, Sarah's slave Hagar--the daughter of the pharaoh--bore Abraham a son named Ishmael. Ishmael is said to be the father of the Muslim world.

Rebekah, who had shown kindness at the city well to Abraham's servant Elizeu, married Isaac and had two children, Jacob and Esau, who also became the fathers of nations. Jacob is another father of the ation of Israel and it's said that the Romans were the descendants of Esau.

And then there is the story of Rachel. Jacob worked for her father for seven years in order to be able to marry her only to have to work another seven years after being tricked into marrying Rachel's older sister Leah.

I think you'll agree that Esther is an interesting person in the Bible. After all, she has her own book! So what was Esther's contribution to mankind?

Esther was a good and obedient wife to Ahasuerus, the king of Persia. Unlike his previous wife, Vashti, who scorned him in front of his buddies and was expelled from the court, Esther helped her people, the Jews, regain their place in history and stopped the abuse they were subjected to. Mordecai, her uncle, was made a dignitary at king's court because of her.

Was this a small role? Maybe, but with historic consequences.

And who doesn't know the story of how Delilah the Philistine betrayed Samson? How foolish of Samson to take a wife from a foreign land and disobey his own parents for her!

Certainly, Delilah was not taken from Samson's rib—she wasn't obeying him, she was obeying her family.

What a beautiful example Ruth is, for staying with her husband's mother, Naomi, even after her husband's death. By refusing to go to her family and following Naomi into her land, Ruth re-marries and gives birth to a nation.

What about Dorcas, who was sewing coats for the poor, and was so loved that her followers intervened with the Apostle Peter to have her resurrected from death?

And what about Mary, the young virgin whom God chose to give birth to our Savior, Jesus Christ?

What about Mary and Martha of the New Testament and their devotion to our Lord Jesus Christ? "For Mary has chosen that which is most important and will not be taken away from her,"--the love and worship of our Lord.

We all know the story of how Mary spilled the expensive perfume to wash our Lord's feet and dry it with her long hair. She knew it was really for his burial.

All of these are admirable examples of women who, playing the roles of wives and mothers, gave birth to nations!

Small roles? Maybe.

But what would humankind be today without the small contributions of women?

I hope that I've made my point with these examples: there is beauty in the role of helper.

Gifts.

The books of Matthew describe the three magi from the east bringing baby Jesus three gifts upon his birth: gold, Frankincense and myrrh, thus predicting the new born's future: a kingdom, priesthood, and a painful death.

The legend of the godmother fairies giving gifts to a new born is common throughout the entire world and also in Romania.

When a child is born, parents and godparents present the child with few things like a book, a pencil, a shiny piece of jewelry, a piece of cloth, etc.

The first item that the child reaches for predicts their future profession or way of life.

Well, nobody ever told me what I chose at my birth, or even if anybody performed the ritual, but the first memory I have as a child, less than 1 year old, is this:

My parents bought a grand house with ornate stucco ceilings and trim, big airy rooms, and gleaming hardwood floors. A balcony with huge flower vases hung from the second floor and I remember a beautiful glass canopy over the front door.

The house belonged to two sisters who gladly sold it because they dreamt of separate lives and quarters.

My first memory as a child was that my parents were negotiating to sell the house to somebody else because they'd hit hard times, just like the rest of the country.

I understood what was going on and I feared for my security and shelter.

I kept busy crawling on the floors and writing on the walls, scribbling all around the great room that had once been the ballroom of the house.

The transaction must have fallen through because we remained in the house.

The winters in Romania are cold and the only heating sources were the tall ceramic stoves in the corner of each room. My father used to light a fire in each stove every day, sometimes with wood logs, but more often with charcoal. Despite the warm stoves, it was always cold, especially in the old ballroom.

It was so cold in the great room during winter that we'd store food there to preserve it.

Those were in the days before refrigerators.

One day, after I'd started school, my teacher came to pay us a visit to see how we lived.

My parents were both teachers and we were all home alone.

The teacher entered the big room up front and there were plates with food (fried beans, my father's favorite) and different pots and pans around the room as if the roof was leaking.

She didn't say anything and left, and I remember how embarrassed I was.

It's true that the more you spend on something the more attached you become to it.

Over the years we spent a lot of money, time, and hard work to fix the old house and bring her back to her former glory, only to leave everything behind, and move to another part of the world.

I don't regret it; I have fond memories of the old grandiose house in Romania.

Later on, I started to write, this time on paper or my keyboard instead of the walls. I became a writer.

So, maybe there is something true about the old custom of godmothers and fairy tales.

For sure, I chose the pencil!

Cazemata

BUCHAREST, ROMANIA, 1950S

I remember it clearly as if it was yesterday. It was summertime. I was a little girl, maybe six or seven, with curly hair, wearing a pink-and-white checked ruffled dress. It was one of my favorites.

We children were playing in the back yard. We had great trees in the back yard, half of them dead.

My brother, Radu, two years younger than me, had built himself a military pillbox; he called it his *cazemata*. It was built between two huge dead trees along the wall of the neighboring house. His pillbox had a flat tin roof and two big flapping pieces of charcoal-colored military tent as the door entrance. I remember it as a black compound, which I was forbidden to enter.

Nevertheless, one time I ventured to the entrance and noticed that it was very strategically built. From the entrance you could see the wrought-iron front gate of our house and the street. Radu and his friends--boys only--were playing "hotii si vardistii," or cops and robbers.

We girls played played with dolls in the other half of the back yard, away from the boys. We set up houses for our dolls in an empty suitcase that I dragged from the house. I had a little cooking stove, pans, and a little table. I remember cleaning up my doll's house, pretending I was all grown up with a family of my own, the Lady of the house.

I played with my friends Louisa and Simona, the daughters of one of our tenants, and other neighborhood girls.

My sister, Mady, two years older, was already attending school. Mady used to bring home books from her friends or from the school, or from the school's library, and I read them avidly—I'd read everything she brought home, everything I could get my hands on. Reading books was like escaping into an imaginary world, where I could become whoever I wanted to be.

So, I had an answer ready when we younger girls started talking, "What would you like to be when you grow up?"

I remember answered with no hesitation, "I want to be a *boieroaica,* a wealthy woman (the word probably derives from the French word *bourgeoisie*.) Now remember, we're talking about the 1950s in Communist Romania. However, I had figured out that if I were to be a *boieroaica,* servants would attend to my every need; I'd be pampered and loved and have a good life. What could be better?

Only... I could see in front of my eyes a picture from a book I was reading of a young girl fixing up and cleaning a run-down house, bringing light inside. Now, that was something that I would also like to do. To clean and fix up and bring light and order to a place of my own. A different picture all together from the *boieroaica* that I had imagined myself, but still appealing, nevertheless.

***

And after so many years, I look back. Were my dreams fulfilled? I think I was more of a servant that a master, but nevertheless, I led a more fulfilling life than I could have imagined.

12

Focsani,

FOCSANI ROMANIA 1950S

I remember when I was five years old or so taking a bath in a little aluminum pan that my aunt Maria had set outside in the garden among tall, fragrant, yellow wildflowers, at her house in Focsani.

It was summer and my brother Radu and I had been left at Aunt Maria's house for the summer.

I don't remember my older sister, Mady (short for Magdalena), being with us. Maybe she stayed back in Bucharest with our parents. My parents were both professors and on vacation at the time, but they were probably occupied with cleaning and painting our old house in Bucharest. (I know that after one summer, I came home to find the big house in Bucharest freshly painted, with a new, intricate, golden design on the walls.)

My Aunt Maria, the older sister of my father, did not have children and lovingly agreed to keep us for summer.

The old house belonged to my grandparents on my father's side, both dead. There were pictures of an imposing man with a moustache, my grandfather Jirca, and a matronly woman, my grandmother Lina, all over the house. (Now looking back at these pictures, I realized that my sister Magdalena looks a lot like my grandmother Lina.)

My grandfather had been in the business of buying and selling fresh fruits and vegetables and also had a small jam factory. The old factory building was located just across the old cobblestone street from their house.

I remember playing with the neighbors' children, especially a boy named Dan, who took a fancy to me. We'd play in the deserted jam factory, hiding in the huge, empty barrels.

The street was appropriately called "Two Pecan Trees Street." The house had two great rooms up front on either side of the entrance as well as a series of rooms on one side, the last one being the kitchen, with doors that opened to a deep, covered porch. In summer breakfast was served at a table on the porch.

In the front yard was a garden full of colorful wildflowers, and in the back was a huge pecan tree. The latrine was also outside in the back yard.

The house and neighborhood were part of the old Focsani before the Communists demolished everything and replaced the charming old buildings with five or six story apartment buildings, all practically identical, but with indoor plumbing.

Breakfasts were always a treat, because Maria's husband, Costian, would be at work, and we children could enjoy the company of our aunt, and listen to old stories about our grandparents. We admired the table with its immaculate, embroidered tablecloth and napkins, silver egg holders, silver teaspoons, homemade bread and butter, and boiled eggs done to perfection (one needs to count to 200 after the water starts to boil).

In the evenings, Costian joined us for dinner on the porch. I remember my Aunt Maria as a lovely and loving lady, but my Uncle Costian was an old gentlemen. He was always very neatly dressed, wearing a red bow tie, his wavy white hair neatly combed, and his eyes a young, startling blue.

One evening my brother Radu and I started laughing about Costian's nose, that we thought resembled a pickle jar. We were laughing uncontrollably, and Costian took offense. Radu, age three, ran to the back yard and climbed on top of the latrine. Costian followed, waving his cane. I pleaded with Radu to stop laughing and come down, but he would not obey. Maybe he was afraid of Costian's cane.

Later that night, I could hear Maria and Costian loudly fighting in their adjacent bedroom. I guessed it was about us children.

That was the last summer we spent at the house. In the night, Maria had a stroke. She went on to live another sixteen years in the care of her younger sister, Olga, but our vacations with her were a thing of the past.

The Better Chef

BUCHAREST, ROMANIA, 1950S

One morning, Radu and I were home alone. It was winter. The winters could be very cold in Bucharest; sometimes it snowed pretty heavily.

Radu and I were in the small room, the children's room, adjacent to my parents' big bedroom where it was warm. We had ceramic stoves in each room, and Father started the fire in ours every morning before he and Mother left for work. He used charcoal, and the room stayed warm for the day.

At that time, we didn't have any helpers around the house, so we were alone all day. Later, mother found Vica, a young country girl who took care of us while Mother and Father, both professors, were at school.

Now, a trade is something that one steals from a master by watching, if one is interested in learning. That was how Radu and I learned to cook: by watching Mother.

Mady wasn't interested in learning to cook. In fact, she never learned. But after she left for school, Radu and I thought we'd compete against each other for the title of the "best chef." We decided that each should bake a torte, and at the end we would judge whose torte was better.

A torte was something mother baked on special occasions because it's quite complicated to make from scratch. You have to whip the eggs with as many tablespoons of sugar as you had eggs, then add flour (also as many tablespoons as eggs), and then bake it in the oven for about one hour. Finally, after all that, the final step is to dress it with icing, which we also made from scratch from sugar and water boiled until caramelized, and, if desired, a tablespoon of cocoa. Then after the syrup cooled, you had to beat it with a wooden spoon until it solidified before spreading it over the cake.

The process is still quite complicated even today when I bake it.

I took the cake plate and started to work on my cake. My brother was left without a torte plate and decided to set his torte on a wooden board. I thought I'd have an advantage over him from the start, because I had taken the ornate plate. How wrong I was, because Radu's torte ended up being better, higher, and tastier.

The word was out: Radu had made the better torte and to this day, he remains the better chef.

Mother's School
End of Year Party

BUCHAREST, ROMANIA, 1950S

The end of the school year was always a big celebration for both students and professors and marked the beginning of summer vacation.

It was the custom at that time that the teachers' children were invited to the party and given gifts (a nice way to recognize the contribution of their parents).

Mother dressed us up in nice outfits that her friend, Margareta Constantine, also a teacher, had hand-embroidered. (Margareta was a spinster with no children of her own, and the word around town was that she was fond of my father.)

Radu, who was about three or four at the time, was all dolled up in a blue, one-piece embroidered costume. He was chubby, with long, curly blond hair, and little brown boots.

One by one the children ascended to the stage of the theater at Mother's school and recited a poem, and each received a present.

When Radu's turn came, he courageously climbed the stairs. *Radu does not know any poem that I know of,* I thought. *What will he do?*

Radu stood tall in the middle of the stage and started to loudly recite:

"It rains, it rains,

In a new home,

The old women ('Babele')

Sit and lay eggs!

That's it, now give me my bag!" Radu announced.

The entire room exploded with laugher, because the so-called poem was something of a street poem, definitely not suitable for a celebration of school. I had no idea where my brother had heard it.

They presented him with a huge brown bag, bigger than he was, full of candies and cookies and other sweet treats.

And Radu descended the stage, proud and full of himself, hugging the brown bag closely.

Mother and I were mortified.

This story is part of my published book: "Short Stories: The Story of a Refugee".

The Doll

BUCHAREST, ROMANIA, 1950S

For as long as I can remember, I've loved dolls.

I remember playing dolls and house with my friend Louisa in the back yard of our house in Bucharest. My friend Louisa and her family rented a small building toward the back of our house. Not the big one: that one was rented by Madame Sandulescu and her husband and they always acted as if the back yard belonged exclusively to them. A lilac bush in the back yard bloomed beautifully every spring, and a thick vine spread over a wooden frame like a roof, making a perfect place to have lunch or dinner. The Sandulescu family enjoyed the back yard and often had grilled fish over an open fire and ate beneath the vine ever evening and Sundays at lunchtime.

Every time we children went to the back yard to play it was as if we were intruding even though it was our property. But during the weekdays, when Sandulescu was working in the neighborhood shoe repair shop, and his wife was helping him, my friend Louisa and I, and sometimes her sister Simona, played house. I would drag an old suitcase from inside and arrange the interior of it like a regular house.

We had doll furniture and a doll stove and doll pans, and we would make dresses for our dolls, play house, clean up the house, and cook for the dolls, as real mothers would do for their children. I would carry my doll around in the carriage and Louisa would do the same. I do not remember my sister ever participating. It was mainly me and Louisa.

Later, Louisa's mother, Margareta, died unexpectedly, and her family moved back to Timisoara, where her father's family came from. I lost my friend and never played house again.

I remember seeing a doll in Tincutza's house, in Ploiesti, which I had my heart set on. This doll was the first doll I'd seen that closed her eyes and could say "Mama". She was the size of a small child, all dressed up in a long purple gown with beige laces. We children were not allowed to play with her; we had to be content just to look.

One summer we were coming back from a summer vacation with our parents. I do not remember exactly how old I was at the time. I remember that for some reason, my parents promised me that when we got back from vacation, we would stop first in Ploiesti, to see my Uncle Gorg, and they would give me Tincutza's doll.

We were traveling by train, and when we arrived at the train station and I recognized the train station as Bucharest and not Ploiesti, I refused to go on the Tram to go home. I remained on the train platform, crouched down, and started to cry and yell. A big crowd formed immediately around me, and my parents could do nothing. I was very frustrated about the doll, but more upset because my parents had lied to me. Usually, I was a quiet child who liked more to observe than to act, and in under other circumstances, I would have been mortified by my behavior. But at the time I was enraged beyond comprehension.

I never got Tincutza's doll, but when I was about fourteen years old, in Bucharest, we went to the first post-war German Exhibit and my father promised me he would buy me a doll that closed her eyes. He probably remembered my heart break over Tincutza's doll. I was a big girl, going to high school by then, but I remember being so excited about the prospect of father buying me a doll that I talked myself into not being so excited. I thought if I wished for something so much, I might not get it. Something would go wrong, and I would not get the doll. But father kept his promise and took me to the German Exhibit and bought me a doll with curly blond hair and blue eyes that closed as I moved the doll. I cherished that doll, and made clothes for her and set her up on my bed and looked at her. Later, when I left Romania, my mother sent me the doll. I took it with me on the airplane from Greece to the USA. I thought if I carried instead of packing it away, it wouldn't be damaged. On the contrary, keeping it there unprotected, the doll was damaged going through customs and when I changed airplanes at JFK in New York on the way to Jacksonville.

I still have a doll from Romania. It is a "tarancutza", a doll dressed in traditional Romanian country clothing, which I have had since childhood. I still have it on a shelf in my bedroom in Jacksonville.

As I heard later from her sister, Louisa married when she was seventeen years old. I, on the other hand, did not get married, and did not have any children.

This story is part of my published book "Short Stories: The Story of a Refugee"

Calarasi

BARAGAN, ROMANIA, LATE 1950S

My father's youngest brother, Costica, was a very tall, handsome, distinguished man, with a military bearing. Before World War II he had been a navy commander on his own ship and earned medals and distinctions in battles.

After the war and after the Communist regime took hold in Romania, he was forced to leave his house in Turnu Severin, on the Danube River, and was forced to move to Baragan, overnight.

Now, Baragan was the equivalent in Romania of Siberia in Russia: a place of hardship in the middle of swamps and desolate fields, isolated from the civilized world.

Costica was married at that time to Ileana, and they had a small girl about my age, Roxana. Ileana came from an aristocratic family (her maiden name was Coanda) and had inherited a small palace in Turnu Severin. Ileana was my uncle's second wife. His first wife was from Focsani and was a young, beautiful French woman. Costica had loved her very much. But the young wife could not live with a Navy husband, and during her husband's prolonged absences, she ran away with a local pharmacist. Then, Costica married Ileana who was a few years older and not as pretty as his first wife, but she had all the education, manners and rigorous upbringing of her social class. Ileana had never had to work on her life. Her parents always had plenty of servants to do everything for her.

Costica, Ileana and their daughter, Roxana, had to move overnight from their house in Turnu Severin with very few of their belongings.

After the move, my uncle used to say that if he had known where "they" were taking them, then taking a shovel and an axe from their home would have been a smarter choice than some of the silver. ("They" being the Communist regime and their Secret Service called "Securitate").

On a summer vacation during the late 1950s, I was invited to visit them in Baragan. Father put me into the train in Bucharest, along with our yellow bicycle, and my uncle waited for me at the train station in Calarasi. Looking back, I think I was the only one from the extended family to visit them in Baragan. When I got there, they made a house for themselves. It was not a great house, but it was one you could live in. I don't remember precisely, but I think it was made of "kirpici"--clay straw walls and a grass roof, because was no forest in Baragan to supply wood. It had two rooms and dirt floors; my uncle built it with his own hands. First, as I understand the process, they had to dig what was called a "bordey" into the ground to serve as the foundation for the shelter, and then they built the house above. There were no other houses nearby, or other people, that I recall. Of course, I was a child at the time, but I don't remember thinking of it as a place of total desolation. On the contrary, to me it was a rustic and picturesque place; the open fields were beautiful and the house itself was joyous, and they had the best bacon I've ever eaten. Ileana, who never had to do anything in her life, adjusted perfectly; or at least I never heard her complaining about anything. She loved my uncle and did whatever she could to help. She learned how to cook and do the laundry, and probably a lot more than I could imagine. She took care of all of them. Between the two of them, she was the backbone of their marriage, the unsinkable one. Their daughter, Roxana, my cousin, studied at home with her mother, and she spoke French much better than me who was studying in school in Bucharest.

Later, they were allowed to move out of Baragan, and went to Braila, once again on the Danube River. I visited them again on another summer vacation, after they'd moved into a rented house in Braila. I remember going fishing with them on the Danube. Both Ileana and Roxana loved to fish and loved the water.

My uncle found employment as an engineer, and the family later on brought a flat in Galati. After the Communist regime fell in Romania in 1989, Roxana tried and succeeded in getting her family possessions back. She also got back the house in Turnu Severin. The irony is that now the largest airport in Bucharest is named "Henry Coanda" after a famous air industry pioneer, and a close relative of Ileana.

Liviu

BUCHAREST, ROMANIA, 1950S

I remember being a small girl attending Elementary Scholl in Bucharest, Romania.

My family house was located near the center of Bucharest, a five minute walk from the Cismigiu Gardens and Calea Victoriei, the main central street, and my school.

The Elementary School in our neighborhood was adjacent to the biggest Catholic Cathedral in Bucharest, the Saint Joseph Cathedral. The adjacent buildings probably once belonged to the cathedral, but under the Communist regime they'd been transformed into classes. The school also had a fairly large yard.

My first teacher was Miss. Purcareanu, an older, plump lady, nicely dressed and always nicely made up. I remember her because she was very partial to the students whose mothers would bring her small gifts. One time, I remember, one of the mothers brought her a big cake that she took it home and did not share it with us children.

Miss Purcareanu wanted to find any especially gifted children among us by testing out our singing capabilities. One day she called me in front of the class to lead a song, but I wasn't a talented singer--she pushed me aside immediately after I started! Taken by surprise by the blunt gesture, I fell on the ground and the whole class burst out laughing. I did not like her!

My second elementary teacher was an older man named Mr. Sfetcu (later I heard that he used to drink excessively). Anyhow, he liked to play the violin and would teach us songs while he played. I don't know how appropriate the songs were for children under ten, but I remember his songs to this day.

One time, when he was sick, he asked my father to teach in his place. Both my parents were teachers--my father was a mathematics professor.

My father called on me to come to the black; he called me by my last name, and I startled, not recognizing my own name when my father used it. He asked me to do a three digit multiplication problem. I remember scratching the numbers quickly on the black board. I excelled in mathematics, of course, and also in calligraphy because my father kept a careful eye on my writing (do you remember the ink pens, not the automatic ones, but the old ones you dipped in an ink well?)

We had a mixed class as the Communists believed in equality between the sexes, and I was seated next to a boy named Liviu.

Now, the other girls were attracted to the mean boys, the boys that were starting fights, and were using crude language, but Liviu was a gentle, well-behaved boy. He was exceedingly considerate and never participated in fights. I was 7 or 8 years old, but I was surely in love with Liviu. He was not handsome in the usual way: he had black hair, parted on one side, a dark complection, a longer nose, chocolate eyes, and--as I remember to this day--he had a dark spot in the white of one of his eyes (obviously, I stared quite a lot into his eyes!)

I loved him in secret, of course, and we never spoke. I was just content to sit next to him, feeling safe and liked. Really, I had no idea if he liked me, but he accepted me. Maybe we said a few words once in a while. Liviu was sure of himself, centered, not trying to impress me, or anybody else for that matter. But he also wasn't and never asked for approval.

We had a country girl who lived with us, Vica, who took care of us while my parents were working. Vica would dress me for school, and arranged my long, chestnut hair in two braids that she tied on the top of my head like a crown. We didn't wear uniforms in elementary school--that came later in middle School. I had a white blouse and a green skirt with white polka dots. I thought I looked like a mushroom when I dressed in them.

When I finished elementary school, I changed schools to the middle school that was located just around the corner. Saint Sava, or Sava, was the best school in all of Bucharest. SAVA used to be a boys' school before the Communists. At that time, Sava was a middle school and a high school with 5th grade to 11th grade. As I changed schools, I never saw, or heard from Liviu again.

Our love was lost, but not in my memory.

Years after, when the Communist regime in Romania fell, I returned to Bucharest to visit my house and my schools. The building complex that once was the elementary school belonged to the Catholic church, and now the entire placed was fenced and the gate locked. Sava has become a college and once again access was restricted; the front iron gate had a security guard and I wasn't allowed in.

The Delights and Pitfalls of Reading

BUCHAREST, ROMANIA, 1950S

I was about ten or eleven, wearing my school uniform, a black and white checked dress with a black ruffled apron, a white band holding back my hair. I was roaming through the great library of the old school, Sava, that I attended back in Romania.

Sava used to be an exclusive boys school, but now under the Communist regime, girls and boys were equal, taking all the same classes.

The great library was filled with books from the wood floors covered with an old Persian rug to the ceiling. The books, the furniture, the rug--even the old distinguished librarian--were all remnants of the old regime, the old school.

Nobody was there but the old gentleman sitting at his desk, deeply immersed in his reading. The classics were lined up on one side of the room. *I have read all of them,* I thought as I walked slowly past. Stendhal's *The Red and the Black*, Theodore Dreiser's *Sister Carrie*, Dostoyevsky's *The Brothers Karamazov*, Tolstoy's *Anna Karenina*. All beautiful books, soul-enriching books.

Now, I wanted to check out Flaubert's *Madame Bovary*. With the book in my hand, I timidly approached the old gentleman.

He took the book from me and looked at me with disbelief. I was in 5th grade at the time, a tiny girl, pale and timid. "That's something you shouldn't read," he said.

Then he looked at a list of all the books I'd checked out over time. "None of these are appropriate for your reading. They are not in your class requirements. You should read *Don't Forget Darrie* or other books recommended by your teacher, not these."

I didn't say anything, but stayed there with my book in my hand, silently pleading to take the book with me.

He looked at me again, and took pity. "Your parents should look at what you read," he said, but he let me borrow the book.

How could he know that reading was my whole world? I could read and forget everything about the ordinary life that I lived, about the things we had to do without, about Mother who had to work and raise three children, about the food shortage, about the big old house that needed a new roof, about the noisy tenants, one family per room, who were imposed upon us once the Communist regime was installed.

Reading was my refuge, my paradise. I could immerse myself in a book and live the life of the book's heroine, pretending, dreaming.

I spent the night before a test reading *Gone with the Wind* well past midnight. I could recite from memory whole passages and dialogue from the books I loved.

Reading can be addictive. Books became my reality, and the *real* reality became foggy, just a waiting period until I could retire in my room and read again.

Later, when I started to write myself, writing was like a force greater than I could have imagined. I had to express myself in writing. All my thoughts, all my feelings had to come into the light.

And so I started to find ways to learn how to write. I felt like a sculptor who dreamed of building the masterpiece of his life and had no tools to do it with. I had to find the tools.

I started a series of classes on novel writing offered by *Writer's Digest*. It was a one-on-one correspondence class where an experienced writer looked over my writing and guided me, corrected me, and taught me.

They paired me with Meredith, a writer from California. What a wonderful experience! How grateful I was for her constructive criticism and for her generosity in sharing with me everything she knew about writing.

Then I took a class on poetry writing, "Poets Laureates," offered by the International Library of Poets and Poetry.com.

Now, these classes had spoiled the pleasure of reading for me.

Let's take a contemporary author that I admired and whose books I wished to emulate. I started to analyze what I read and tried to figure out how she'd done it, what techniques she'd used, so I could learn.

Soon enough, I discovered that in all her books she was used basically the same three characters, three women, with the same character traits, that she put in different circumstances. But the plot and the characters were basically the same.

Then I thought how true Stephen King's remark was: "I cannot write another book; I keep repeating myself." One writes about what one knows. You draw from your own experiences, feelings, and thoughts and there are so many new things you can add. Then you start repeating yourself.

Not so with the classics. Those are books you can read and read again and still find something new, something that can enrich and touch your very soul. And that is the difference between a good book and a masterpiece.

But reading has spoiled something far more important for me: it spoiled my life, my romantic life, I mean. Over the years no one could quite measure up to the highly idealized heroes of my beloved books.

So, the old gentleman, the librarian, was right after all. *Madame Bovary* was very inappropriate reading for a sensitive eleven-year-old.

Now I'll tell you a story about my mother, Thiana, and her childhood in Avdela, her beloved native village in Greece.

The Viper

AVDELA, GREECE, 1920S

(This is part of my book called Thiana-AVDELA-A Macedonian Village in Northwestern Greece-Thiana's Native Land, iUniverse,2003.)

Thiana and her sister, Maritza, gathered pinecones in the woods. Their mother had sent them early in the morning with two big sacks. She needed pinecones and wood to heat up the *chireap* (the outside fireplace). It was Friday, the day to bake bread.

Thiana was only six at the time, a tiny girl with curly, chestnut hair cut short to the earlobes. Maritza was nine. She had thick, curly, ash-blond hair and a round face that seemed to be smiling all the time. The girls were barefoot.

Thiana saw it first. It slid out from the bushes beside the pine-needle-covered path she was walking as she searched for cones. It was a snake, a viper.

Thin as a finger, it was gray, with a flat head, with a black V on the top. For a moment, Thiana stood transfixed. It seemed the viper stared at her too. Thiana opened her mouth to call her sister, but no sound came out. Like a bolt of lightning, the viper bit her bare foot and slithered away again

Thiana fell unconscious.

Maritza heard her sister tumble to the ground and ran to see what had happened. Thiana's eyes were shut, her left foot red and starting to swell.

Maritza dropped her sack of pinecones and ran, as fast as she could, skirts in hand, back to the village.

"Help, somebody help my sister!" she screamed, as soon as she reached the outskirts of the village.

A man ran out of his house. "Hey, Maritza, what happened?"

"My sister, Thiana, she is in the woods, unconscious. I think a viper bit her foot—it's swelled up, and all red. Quick, help her!"

"I'll come with you. Stella," he called to his wife, "Let everyone know, what happened. Try to find her father and bring him to the woods."

"Father isn't home yet," said Maritza. "He's supposed to be back today."

The man ran back in the woods with Maritza. When they found Thiana, she was still lying on the ground, unconscious, her left foot badly swollen.

"Help me hold her leg up," the man told Maritza. "I can see the two holes the viper's teeth left in her heel. I'll try to suck the venom."

The man put her little sister's heel to his mouth and sucked out the blood, mixed with the viper's venom, then spat it on the ground next to him.

"Try to hold her leg still on my thigh. Be sure she doesn't move," the man said kneeling next to Thiana.

Maritza took her sister's leg on her arms and held it as tightly as she could, on the man's thighs. He took out of his back pocket a knife, opened the blade, and wiped it across his thigh.

He started to cut away at Thiana's heel. Blood poured onto the pine needles and leaves which covered the ground.

The village men came and stood around in a circle.

"Somebody give me a chain to tie her leg with," the man said.

"Here, I knew you'd need this." Another man handed him a thick iron chain.

The man tied Thiana's ankle with the chain so the infected blood would not get to her heart.

The foot swelled more and more. Everything they knew had been done. Now, it was up to God to save her.

Thiana was still unconscious. Even the sharp pain of the knife cutting into her flesh had not wakened her.

The man took her in his arms and brought her home.

By that time Thiana's father, Iani, had come home. When he saw his daughter, he immediately went outside and killed a young lamb. He put Thiana's foot inside the belly of the freshly slaughtered lamb. The foot was swollen badly, and people were talking of amputation.

The next day, when Thiana woke up, her parents took her foot out of the lamb and washed it. Her leg seemed miraculously healed, white instead of red, and back to normal size.

She was saved.

Communication Or
The Lack Of It...

1980S, ATHENS, GREECE

(This story is part of my book ATHENS, iUniverse, 2004)

I was twenty-five when I left my parents' house in Romania for Greece. Nobody told me that my new status as an immigrant would diminish my status as a human being, would affect my dignity and would badly bruise my ego.

For the first three months after my arrival in Athens, I lived with my cousins.

My cousin Nuly, a dark, handsome man of twenty-five, was still living at home with his parents. He managed to enjoy a careless life even though he worked two jobs. He had a lot of friends, young men and women his age, and they went to taverns almost every evening, staying out until late at night. I could hear him coming back home in the small hours of the night. I was curious to know what he was up to with all that running around.

One evening he offered to take me with him. I was eager to see the city, and the nightlife and his friends. That's how I met George, Nuly's friend.

The first time I met George, my heart skipped a beat. George was a very beautiful man. (Yes, there is such a thing as a beautiful man, believe me.) I liked his red hair and beard, but especially his piercing blue eyes, which I took as a sign of intelligence.

Apparently, George liked me too because he started to invite me out.

One Saturday, he invited me to go to the beach to go on a boat ride. He was to pick me up at my cousins' house around noon after he finished his work. I dressed for the beach with a red tank top and flowery skirt over my bathing suit. On the way, he took a detour and stopped at his house. It was a grand house: two or three stories high, close to the sea, a villa. He invited me in to wait for him to change.

I waited in the entrance hall, sitting on a sofa and admiring the marble floor and staircase, the ornate full-length mirror and furniture.

I was checking myself in the mirror, when a heavy woman with coke-bottle glasses and bad teeth entered the room and stared at me. I knew it must have been George's mother.

George followed shortly and sat next to his mother, both staring at me as if I were an insect pinned on cardboard. I started to question my choice of clothing.

Now, at the time, I could not speak Greek or English even though I understood both. (This is the second step in learning a foreign language; you understand, but cannot speak.)

George's mother said to her son in Greek, "Do not bring this one home every day now, as if you were to take her for your bride."

The son looked at me as if he was weighing me and did not say one word. They were not talking to me; they were talking about me, and examining me, as if I were made of wax. Obviously, they thought I could not understand what they were saying. Never in my entire life had anyone been so rude to me right to my face. I stared back at them angrily and said nothing.

Then George's father came in, a tall, dark, and handsome man. He extended his hand to greet me, and in fluent English apologized. That soothed my ruffled feathers a little, and soon I left with George.

George kept his promise and we went on a boat ride on the Mediterranean Sea. The boat ride, the sea, the sunset--it was all like a dream, if I had been in the mood to dream. But my dreams had been brutally shattered by George's mother's remarks about me.

When we returned to George's home to bring back the boat, George invited me in again. This time I refused; I said that I would wait for him in the car.

His mother came up on the balcony and tried to invite me in. She even sent George's sister down to talk to me. But the humiliation I'd endured earlier burned red-hot in my heart and my mind and I would not budge.

George got me safely home that night, and I think that was the last I saw of him.

Monday morning, I went to my other uncle, who had a pastry shop in Platia Omonia, and told him the entire story. I was crying, but my uncle was unsympathetic. "You were pretty stupid to cross his mother!" he told me. "The boy would not do anything without his mother's approval. You should have played the fool, as if you did not understand her remark, and smiled, and been friendly. That's how you do it."

Too bad, I could not get over my pride. Who knows, maybe now, I could have become the fat woman with coke-bottle glasses looking down to my future daughter-in-law, in a beautiful Villa on the Mediterranean, instead of stubbornly trying for an engineer manager promotion in Jacksonville, Florida.

Blame it on communication, or the lack of it!

The Bird

ATHENS, GREECE, 1980

(This story is part of my book ATHENS, iUniverse, 2004.)

I n 1980 I spent fourteen months in Greece, hoping against hope that I would be allowed to stay.

I was working on my immigration papers as well as my English as I attended the Hellenic-American Institute in Athens Greece.

After my relatives kicked me out for overstaying my welcome, I rented a small efficiency apartment, a *garsoniera*, on the first floor of a sturdy, five-story building located at the toe of Licavitos hill in the middle of Athens.

I loved the *garsoniera immediately—it had a small kitchen area, a bathroom, and an airy, medium-sized room with polished hardwood floors and a French door opening on a small balcony.* The building was ve ry well-kept and clean, in sharp contrast with everything else I'd seen. And the rent was the same as others charged, about 5,000 drachmas (around fifty dollars) a month.

But my biggest luck was to meet and become friends with Theresa.

Theresa and her mother owned the building. Theresa was the daughter of a former Greek general, and had been highly educated abroad.

At the time I was in Athens, Teresa and her husband Vasili had had some family problems. Vasili had moved with another woman to Patra, while Teresa, her mother, and her daughter Rania, remained in Athens.

I spent many days and evenings with Teresa and her family. They became my "away from home family." I learned how to speak Greek, and Teresa, who had influential connections, helped me with my immigration papers.

Teresa's family had a bird, a multicolored parrot with bright yellow and deep blue plumage, called Vasili, after Teresa's estranged husband.

Evenings, while we sat around the dining table or watched television, Vasili the bird roamed freely through the living room, responding to Theresa's barbs, whistling, and walking out onto the open terrace that wrapped the living room.

One weekend, Teresa and her family went out of town and left the parrot in my care. I was looking forward to spending some fun time with the bird in my little apartment, but it was not meant to be. Vasili did not recognize my voice and did not respond to me. He didn't whistle; he was sad because he missed his own apartment and his people.

Winter can be cold in Athens; it doesn't snow, but it's cold and windy, and at the time heat was in short supply. On Sunday morning, I opened the balcony door and took Vasili's cage out for a major clean-out, as I had seen Teresa do.

Without a second thought, I opened the cage door and let the bird out onto the open balcony in order to change the newspapers, clean the cage, and refresh his water. At first, Vasili did not want to leave his cage; I had to push him out. Then he stood there on the balcony, looking at me, brooding. I did my job: I changed the newspapers, cleaned the cage, changed the water, and expected him to willingly enter his newly cleaned home.

Not so! He had no intention of going back into his cage, and as I prodded him he started to peck at my hands with his big beak.

It was cold outside, despite the sunshine, and I was impatient. I had not had a chance to shower and dress for the day. I hadn't even combed my hair. I was still wearing my long flannel nightgown and bright red, embroidered Chinese slippers my mother had sent me.

Suddenly, I got scared, thinking that the bird might fly away; the balcony was open, after all. Then Teresa would kill me for sure, after she threw me out in the street. I started to panic and pushed Vasili harder toward the cage.

NO WAY!

The bells were ringing at Saint Nicholas Church, down the road; well-dressed people came out on the street below the balcony where I stood in my nightgown, fighting with a parrot.

What was I to do?

Finally, good sense came to me and I carried the cage inside, hoping Vasili would follow. It worked! He liked his house too much to let it get too far away from him. He followed me in and I immediately closed the door.

First round! I'd won!

Now, I thought, came the easy part: I had to coax the bird into the cage, and quickly, as I had big plans for the day and no time to fiddle with a reluctant bird.

But Vasili had different ideas. Instead of going into his cage, he started to follow me around and pinch my feet with his thick, hooded beak.

Now, he was the aggressor, and he was in charge of the situation, like the man he was.

I panicked again and jumped on top of my unmade bed in order to escape Vasili, but Vasili flew right after me and pecked at me feet. (*So he* can *fly*, I was thinking, while I tried to elude him.)

A scene from the Hitchcock's movie *The Birds* came to my mind and I was afraid that the bird was going to go for my eyes next.

In desperation, I snatched my overcoat and ran outside the room, closing the door after me.

Round Two! Vasili Won!

In the hallway outside my apartment, I took a look at myself: the overcoat was knee length; my nightgown was floor length; I still had my red slippers on my feet; and my hair was a mess. *I probably look like a madwoman,* I thought. Nonetheless, I decided to venture outside. It was only a few blocks to the apartment of my aunts Maria and Pipitza. And I really needed help.

What a sight I must have been for the people on the street going to church!

When I arrived at my aunts' apartment, Maria had already left for church, but Pipitza agreed to come back with me to the *garsoniera* and help with the bird.

When we arrived, the room looked like a war zone—bright plumage all over, the bed a mess, and chairs upended from my mad dash for the door. Vasili was pacing the room, angry.

Pipitza approached the bird with outstretched arms, cooing soft words, and a miracle happened: the bird stood still until Pipitza enclosed it in her loving hands.

"This bird is scared to death," Pipitza said reproachfully, "I can feel his beating heart!"

With soothing, childlike words to the bird, Pipitza put it into its cage, locking the gate.

Round Three! Pipitza won!

"What happened?" I wanted to know.

"Let's say you're not a bird person. Birds are like small children: they instinctively know who loves them and who doesn't. Then, you infuriated him with your red fingernails and red slippers," said Pipitza looking sideways at me.

"I didn't know that," was all I could say.

✳✳✳

This story has a moral to it: caring for somebody requires love. Dutifulness is not enough.

The Engagement Party

ATHENS, GREECE, 1980

(This story is also related in my book ATHENS, iUniverse, 2004.)

It happened twenty-something years ago, in another life, in another world, so I feel comfortable telling you the story today.

That summer I was dating Costas. In my heart and in my mind, I was already in love with him. As for Costas? He seemed to be in love with me. He told me as much.

I had met him at Mimis's, where I worked a few months during my stay in Athens. Mimis was the son of my Aunt Pipitza's friend.

A few of us had stayed at the office after work, debating where to go for the evening. Then Costas came in: tall, dark, handsome, impeccably dressed in a dark suit, his dark, curly hair arranged carefully. He was Mimis's friend and worked for him sometimes. Costas was finishing his Master's and had just returned from London. For me it was love at first sight.

Also, he was somebody to practice my English with. So, we started to date and talk and share thoughts and plans.

One weekend in autumn, Mimis invited me to spend the weekend at his villa in Raffia, on the Mediterranean Sea. It was a few weeks before my stay in Greece was to end. I had been accepted at the American Embassy, where they had found me a sponsor in the USA.

I went by bus, for Raffia was maybe 30 kilometers outside Athens.

Mimis was a rich man. He owned a tall, multilevel building right on the beach. When I arrived, late Friday afternoon, the women were preparing for a party. Mimis's wife and his girlfriend (there was talk at the office that Mimis's daughter was really by his married girlfriend rather than his wife) were setting tables and making sandwiches and other finger food. They were speaking rapidly in Greek and I had a hard time keeping up with the conversation. I felt left out, so I went for a swim.

When I returned, the guests were gathering, and the women were now fussing around a young, beautiful girl, preparing her for a *proxenia*, or engagement party. That much I could understand. The girl was related to one of Mimis's women, probably his girlfriend.

Now, you have to understand the custom: in Greece, even today, there are arranged marriages, also called *proxenias*

The families arranged the marriage; the man had to have a job, but the woman had to bring a dowry or *prika* into the marriage.

The night was beautiful with the sea beating at the beach at the foot of the grand building and the stars shining so close that you could catch them with your hand.

I was sitting in a corner, unnoticed, as I did not know anybody at the party besides Mimis, who was too busy to talk to me. He was arranging everything; he was pulling the strings, so to speak. I figured it was fine for me to remain as I was, with my wet bathing suit on, and a tank top and skirt on top, my hair still wet from swimming. Everybody was eating and drinking and having a good, merry time. They were waiting for the *gambrol,* the bridegroom, to make his appearance.

I was sitting by myself in a corner of the large veranda, enjoying the evening, drinking in my last moments in Greece. I felt detached from the happenings around me, my mind on my upcoming trip to the United States and my family back in Romania.

At eleven, the groom appeared. He made his grand entrance by stairway and stood tall in the doorframe. I looked up and could not believe my eyes: it was Costas, my Costas. He passed by me as if I did not exist, and approached the group fussing around the bride.

It was more than I could endure, for I'd had no warning. Mimis had not told why he invited me to Raffia for the weekend. Costas had not mentioned anything about his engagement.

I started to visibly tremble. Mimis's wife, who was an ugly woman that Mimis married for her fortune--at least that was the word that Mimis's girlfriend had spread around the office--noticed and came over with a sweater. I felt trapped, like a mortally wounded animal. My mind ran in overdrive. Raffia was 30 kilometers outside Athens. Busses did not circulate at that time of night. I knew without a doubt that if I were to stay there for the weekend I would die. To be forced to watch Costas with the young girl, pretending nothing was between the two of us, was beyond my ability to handle.

I looked around me for the first time since my arrival, checking all the other guests. At the other corner of the veranda was a fat man, whose wife, I had heard, had just left him. I went over to him and asked if he was willing to take me back to Athens that evening. The man agreed. Perhaps he thought I had designs on him, for he was rich, but he was a gentleman and left me at my aunt's house without incident. There at the door, I collapsed and was sick for a week.

At the end of September, I left for the United States.

I have wondered so many times about what made Mimis invite me to Raffia that weekend knowing that I was dating Costas.

To this day, I still cannot fathom it.

Wakulla Springs

JACKSONVILLE, FLORIDA, 1982

(This story was also told in my book America—The Final Destination, Publish America, 2006.)

My first job, which I got just two months after my arrival in the United States, was with an office of the State of Florida, here in Jacksonville.

Frank, who interviewed me for the job and became my boss, was a man in his late forties or early fifties, small, round, and bald, with a protruding belly and round glasses.

As much as I'd like to believe I got my job based on my qualifications, I have to admit that maybe--just maybe--it had something to do with me being young, female, and reasonably attractive.

Frank was a confirmed bachelor. I found that out later, along with some other disturbing pieces of information.

Now, he no longer works there; he is retired, and I think I'm safe telling you the gossip.

One Monday morning, Frank came in late and very disturbed, his clothes in disarray. I noticed right away, because Frank was usually very impeccably dressed. "What's going on with Frank?" I asked my friend Kathleen.

Kathleen responded with a wide grin on her face. "You mean to tell me you don't know?"

"Know what?"

"Well, Frank visits those nudist colonies, and this past weekend there was a police raid, and they took his clothes away! He had some explaining to do at the police station, and he had to drive back home in the nude."

"What was he doing at a nudist colony?"

"Well, I don't know exactly, but the guys claim he hides behind bushes and spies on the teenage girls over there!"

***

Within the first months of my starting work, Frank and I were sent to give a presentation at a workshop in the Tallahassee office. We had to use an overhead projector and had a tripod and a portable screen with us just in case we needed them.

Frank drove the state-owned car. His secretary made reservations for both of us at the Ramada Inn in Tallahassee.

When we arrived at the hotel, I was upset to find out that Frank and I had adjoining rooms with a connecting door. Before I even put my luggage down, I made sure that the lock and bolt were secured. I was so upset that it gave me a migraine. Maybe the boss had designs on me after all. But there was no way I would accept any advances from my boss.

I decided to behave so that the older man couldn't even open his mouth to say anything out of line. I wouldn't give him a chance.

The soft knock on the front door disturbed my nap. "It's me, Frank. Do you want to go out and eat this evening?"

At first, I was certain that I wouldn't go out with him, but then reconsidered. I was hungry, and we shared the same car.

"Thank you for asking me. I'll meet you in the lobby in half an hour."

We went to a nice restaurant that Frank was familiar with from previous trips. But by the time the waiter asked for our order, my migraine had gotten worse. My head was pulsating with pain.

"I don't think I can eat anything. I have a bad headache."

"Not even something to drink?" Frank asked.

"Maybe a Pepsi, please," I told the waiter.

While Frank enjoyed his dinner and his drink, I sat there miserable, nursing my headache. I couldn't help noticing that when we left, Frank left a small tip and returned afterwards and took some change back. I thought the older man was cheap.

I was glad to get back to my hotel room, where I could be violently sick and go to bed.

The second day we drove to the Wakulla Springs resort just outside Tallahassee, on the Gulf. That was where the State of Florida was holding the three-day workshop.

It was a beautiful resort, built like a castle among pine trees, located on the edge of the Okefenokee Swamp and right on the clear, spring-fed lake. It was an old, picturesque building with a great fireplace in the living room-reception area downstairs. Curved wood stairs led to the upstairs bedrooms. Stained-glass windows overlooked the spring. The sun filtered through the tall windows in the dining rooms, temporarily converted for classes. I could see tourists taking rides in the glass-bottom boats on the spring.

My presentation was scheduled for the afternoon of the first day. I didn't need the overhead projector or the portable screen after all. They had a big screen installed in the classroom and an overhead projector, and everything went smoothly.

There! I was done and now I could enjoy the trip like everybody else.

The next day was Saturday, and we decided that instead of going back to Jacksonville Friday evening, we would stay one more day and visit the swamps.

We paid for the hotel rooms for that night out of our own pockets, and the next day we met with a group of environmental specialists who knew the swamp. We all went in two big 4x4 trucks into the nature preserve. Early in the morning the swamp was enveloped in a thick fog rising from the marshes. We were driving on a narrow path raised above the swamp, and on both sides of the vehicle, alligators swarmed in the muddy water, raising their heads and opening their mouths as we passed. It was the first time I'd seen them, or the other marsh fauna--water snakes, water moccasins, wild turkeys and deer--that make the marshes one of Florida's most valuable resources.

That was a trip to remember.

The Magic of Disney World

FLORIDA, 1990S

Have you ever been burned out to the point that you *know* you need a vacation to recharge your batteries? I'm sure all of you have been there. But, what if you <u>don't have the time or the money, or either (as is usually the case with me), for a full-blown vacation?</u>

For me, a one-day trip to Disney World is all I need to recharge.

Disney World has magic power to awaken the child within you, to make you forget about everything except the next ride.

So, I took one of those "one-day trips" to Disney World. Every local knows that the time to visit the resorts is during the week, not weekends, when the crowds are so thick you cannot see anything. I like to go with my sister and we always fight over which one resort we're going to see with our single precious day off. I prefer Universal Studios, my sister prefers the Magic Kingdom, and both of us like Epcot.

We wake up at 5 a.m., eat a hearty breakfast, and since I'm the designated driver, I make a jar of strong, hot coffee laced with honey (not rum!) for the road.

We have to leave the house around six in the morning to get there at nine, when the resorts open.

The drive is a breeze, with almost no traffic until we get to Orlando. We arrive at the park at nine sharp, dressed comfortably for the day, wearing tennis shoes and of course carrying a camera with plenty of film (this is before digital cameras).

We're ready to start the adventure.

And the adventure will differ depending on which resort we are visiting that day.

If we choose Epcot Center, then the entire trip revolves around the places where we would like to eat. We *have* to start the trip in the Norway Pavilion because they have the best pastries, chocolate cakes, and Danish, plus hot chocolate and coffee for breakfast.

Then we have to plan our journey and places to visit depending on where we decide to eat lunch. Should it be the Mexican restaurant next to the water, where we can oversee the Yucatan Volcano and listen to the sounds of Mexican music, while enjoying the best Mexican food ever eaten? Or will we decide to eat at the Japanese restaurant and sit around the hot table with other guests, enjoying the cooking and the juggling of the Japanese cook and the best beef or shrimp you could imagine? Or how about stopping at the French café to enjoy soup and bread, sitting at the sidewalk tables looking at passers-by?

✳✳✳

Now, the day will be totally different if we decide to go to the Magic Kingdom. There, the food is secondary to the rides. We can stop at practically any time, any place and grab some fast food.

But, which rides, and how many of them you can take, or how to best avoid the crowds and get to the shorter lines, those are the most important things. I like the submarine ride, "20,000 Leagues Under the Sea," and also, "The Haunted Mansion", "The Trek Birds' House," "Tom Sawyer's Island." and the "It's a Small World After All" boat trip and display of dolls from around the world.

Then the 3-D movies, from, *Honey, I Shrunk the Kids* to the formidable Arnold Schwarzenegger's *The Terminator*.

And of course I like Universal Studios for its settings, replicating the Hollywood, California world. (I have never been to California. Not yet, anyhow.) There, you can eat the best pastries on almost any street corner. I always enjoyed the "King Kong" ride, and the subway ride through New York that becomes "Earthquake," and the "Jaws" ride.

We take tons of pictures at every corner.

By 4:00 p.m. we start thinking of heading back. We always say we're going to leave early, but with no exception, there is still that last ride that we're dying to take, and we end up battling the afternoon traffic through Orlando to go back home.

It takes one full hour to drive through Orlando, but the remainder of the trip is clear.

We arrive home exhausted, but so refreshed, ready for work the next day.

It has been a while since my last one-day adventure to Disney World, but just thinking and talking about it is like taking a micro-vacation.

An Attempt to
Understand Engineers

I could not resist the temptation, the gossip temptation …

This one is a little over the edge, but I'll claim the First Amendment on it, and consider my liberty of free speech.

Well, did you hear about the latest scandal at the Capitol, about Congressman Foley, who was visiting and text messaging young, underage pages, instead of attending to his business of being a Congressman?

His poor wife was dangling behind him to save face. And whose face was she trying to save? His or hers? What was she trying to prove? That the Congressman was a faithful family man, or a straight one?

The Speaker of the House, who knew about Foley's whereabouts, did not say one word. He thought to save face. And whose face was he trying to save? The Republican Party's of course!

I suppose the "Love Element" in Congress is very potent. It crosses the political parties' lines, and gender lines, but it is still very potent.

That's where the line becomes a little blurred, because a few years back, as you all recall, it was President Clinton, a Democrat, who was romancing a young intern at the White House.

And what face-saving his wife had to be put through. All to her advantage, as she became stronger, and a powerful Senator herself. One learns from the masters!

Maybe it has to do with the stress of attending to the county's duties. Or, maybe it has to do with the fact that the majority of the Congressmen are lawyers. Yes, it must be a professional thing.

Look at engineers for example. No such thing, no time for love; we carry the world's technology on our shoulders. How many engineers have you heard about text messaging their draftsmen? Maybe only with professional messages.

Engineers are usually the boorish type with round eyeglasses, field boots, and hanging jackets with large, useful pockets.

Here is a tale:

An engineer was crossing the street when a frog tried to catch his attention and spoke to him:

"If you kiss me, I'll transform into a beautiful princess!"

The engineer picked up the frog and deposited it in his large, useful pocket.

The frog yelled more loudly: "Look, if you kiss me I'll stay with you the entire week!"

The engineer took the frog out of his pocket, looked at it, smiled, and then put it back into his pocket.

Then the frog yelled, "Look, if you kiss me, I'll become a beautiful princess, and I'll stay with you for one whole week and do whatever you want!"

The engineer took the frog out of his pocket, looked at it and put it back into his pocket.

Hysterical, the frog cried out, "Didn't you hear? I'm a beautiful princess and I'll make love to you for one week. What's your problem? Why don't you kiss me?"

Irate, the engineer answered:

"Look, I'm an engineer. I do not have time for love, but a talking frog… well, that's something interesting. I think I'll keep you this way!"

So much for engineers' ingenuity!

I think that explains why all the engineers I know, prefer frogs to beautiful princesses.

I told you this one was over the edge! I'll claim the First Amendment on it, or maybe the fifth??

An American Citizen

JACKSONVILLE, FLORIDA 1998

It was my first project management job with the City—the Westside Regional Park.

It was a project of high visibility, in the district of then Councilwoman Tillie Fowler.

I didn't have specific previous experience in working with parks, or parks' design, or railroad crossings. I just had my general expertise as a civil engineer. I worked with a great and talented design consultant team, from Reynolds, Smith and Hills, led by James Turner, their Vice President of Landscaping.

Early on, it became apparent that the project was more complicated than I'd anticipated. It entailed negotiations and coordination with the Naval Air Station, Jacksonville, the owner of the future park's land. It required a new entrance from Roosevelt Boulevard and a new railroad crossing. Environmentally sensitive wetlands were involved. And not the least of all the concerns, an eagle's nest needed to be protected due to federal regulations.

At that point, Councilwoman Fowler felt that it was in the best interest of the project to put somebody with more experience in charge. So, my boss approached me carefully, as he didn't want to upset me, and proposed that somebody with more experience take over, with the provision that I still work on the project.

I don't know if today, knowing all that I know, I would have given the same answer. Now, after thirteen years of working with the city, I have learned better. Now, I might have answered:

"Sure, if I'm still taking home the same salary, let somebody else knock their head on the wall" or,

"If they tell me I cannot do it, then I cannot do it. They know better" or,

"After all I'm a woman. They're right, I'm better suited to stay at home and raise children, than directing engineering jobs and telling men what to do!"

But at that time, my answer was short and not very diplomatic: I gathered the file, which was quite thick, and handed it to my boss. "You take it, and I'm completely out, or you can let me finish the project on time and within budget, with every problem adequately solved."

The next day, my boss told me he'd checked with Councilwoman Fowler, and she indicated that I could finish the job.

That was quite a challenge, but I brought it to a successful conclusion. I'm very proud, even today, of that park, the new entrance, and the new railroad crossing.

But working on the project, I got the chance to know and appreciate our Councilwoman Tillie Fowler. I remember how impressed I was by her quick mind and understanding of all problems, regardless of how technical they were, her diplomacy in achieving agreement in seemingly impossible dealings, and her dignity and poise as she conducted public meetings.

Later on, when Ms. Tillie Fowler went to Washington to become our congresswoman (and I think she did an outstanding job representing the interests of our community) I had to appeal to her to help me with one of my impossible personal problems.

My mother, who came to the US from Romania, along with my brother and sister, in 1986, had put in her application to become an American citizen. What an honor, how proud she was! But dealing with Immigration in Jacksonville and having to pass an oral and written test in American history in order to be able to get her citizenship was another matter.

Mother went to school here and learned English, and we studied hard, my mother, my sister, and I. We pored over the questions and booklets to prepare my mother for the test. Mother was older, and her eyes and her hearing were not good. But she had a determination to learn, and she wanted to become an American citizen.

The first time we went to the examination, the immigration officer was nothing less than rude to her, lacking the patience, or willingness, to hear her out. (I know it for a fact, as I peeked through the cracked door to see if my mother was O.K.) My mother was devastated. The attitude of the officer had a great impact on my mother's morale.

Then, I remembered our Ms. Tillie Fowler in Washington, and I wrote to her to ask for her help with my mother's quest to become an American citizen.

You know what? She remembered me, remembered that I had worked on the Westside Regional Park with her, and she assured me of her support!

And her support came through. My mother was invited at the Immigration office in Jacksonville, and the Commanding Officer himself interviewed my mother, with me in attendance. What a difference in attitude and how that impacted my mother and the way she answered the questions!

What a difference it made in my mother's outlook. She got her most cherished wish; she became an American citizen on the same day. The Commanding Officer swore her in.

I have fond memories of our Congresswoman Tillie Fowler and I, personally, was very disappointed to hear that she succumbed to the outside pressures to step down after only eight years. She was a great Congresswoman and had achieved a lot for Jacksonville and its military population.

Now, the Westside Regional Park is rightfully named: "The Tillie K. Fowler Park" in memory of the late congresswoman.

A Helping Hand

JACKSONVILLE, FLORIDA

I t happened in a glorious sunny Saturday at noon. In our backyard, sunlight filtered through the, thick, over-hanging branches of a magnificent oak, ornate with weeping Spanish moss.

Saturday morning is the designated shopping day in our household. As I approached the back door of the house, the door that opens directly into the kitchen, my arms full of brown bags stuffed with groceries, I heard a "thud," as if a small branch had fallen. I turned to look.

A squirrel had fallen from the tree, a baby squirrel. It didn't move. *Should I get closer and look?* I wondered. *It's not moving. It's probably dead! I don't want to see death up close; even it's a baby squirrel!* I debated, transfixed in place.

The baby squirrel had fallen on its back. *It's strange for a squirrel, even a baby squirrel, to be so stiff. They fly from tree branch to tree branch; I'd even seen them running along telephone wires. They couldn't just fall like that with a thud*, I thought.

Suddenly I saw it moving, trying to turn over, wiggling its tail to help its movement. It stood on its feet now, trembling. The squirrel lifted its head to look at me: eyes like an owl--no, more like a bandit's mask with a pointed nose. Then I realized: *it's not a squirrel, it's a baby raccoon! How cute it is with its owl-like eyes looking straight at me! Is the squirrel asking for my help?*

From the corner of my eye, I saw a big, fat raccoon, probably its mother, climbing down from the oak tree. *I didn't know we had a family of raccoons living in our back yard!*

The big, fat mama climbed down from the tree, her clawed paws hugging the trunk. She posed and looked at me questionably, then she approached her baby—same owl-like eyes, same pointed nose.

For a second as I looked into her eyes, I swear, I could see her pain, the cry for help for her wounded baby.

Then, she carefully, tenderly, took her baby, grabbing it with her mouth by the scruff of its neck, and they both disappeared from view, behind the azalea bush.

Getting hold of myself, I noticed I had not moved. I was still in the same spot, next to the steps to the kitchen, holding the grocery bags in my hands. Could I have helped? Could I have done anything to help? I was still debating in my mind.

***

The next day, a bright, spring Sunday morning, we were having breakfast at the kitchen table; the aroma of strong, hot coffee and freshly toasted bread filled the room. From the glass-paneled door, I could see the new, green leaves of the oak tree, their branches hanging low, dripping with Spanish moss, the fuchsia-colored azalea bush in full bloom, a robin redbreast perched atop, singing its heart out—all God's marvelous creation.

My thought went back to the baby raccoon and the family of raccoons. Cup in hand, I went outside to look for them. But I did not see anything. *Maybe they are having breakfast, right now in the big hole of the oak, just across from the kitchen door.* Had I imagined it, or had I seen the little bandit mask peering straight at me from the tree across from the kitchen door?

After breakfast, fortified and energized, I picked up the tall ladder that we store next to the shed in the back yard and went up front to paint the front porch.

Our home is a Victorian style, two-story, red brick building with white trim that was built somewhere around 1939. It has a front porch with white columns (not the big, grandiose columns you see in Atlanta's big mansions, but on a smaller scale), and a white balcony with a sun deck that we built on top of the Florida room.

The front porch needed painting badly. The magnolia tree that was hanging over the entrance had done a number on the white paint. It looked like it had traces of black ash all over it, like some giant dirty fingers had touched the house and left its ugly marks on it. In reality it was a fungus dripping from the magnolia tree to the house and its white trimming and white front porch. Every time I rake the leathery leaves, I have to remind myself that I bought the house for that magnolia tree. It was the month of May and the magnolia was full of white fragrant flowers.

I balanced the tall ladder on the side on the porch, trying to even its legs on the ground covered with the thick roots of the magnolia tree.

Paint and brush in hand, I started to climb the ladder. It moved, a little, and then a lot!

The next thing I knew, I was sprawled on the ground, the ladder on top of me, white paint everywhere. I could not move. The searing pain stopped my breath.

For a while I stayed there, waiting for the pain to subside. Then I tried my legs to see if I could move them. Yes! Slowly and shakily I rose from the ground taking stock of myself. Nothing broken, only scratches and bruises. I might have to buy another can of paint. I could live with that.

Then my thoughts went back to the day before and the little baby raccoon. With more understanding now I thought, *Yeah, he could've used a helping hand!*

Women in Engineering

JACKSONVILLE, FLORIDA, 2000

In April of 2000, Sheila Widnall, Professor of Aeronautics and Astronautics at MIT and former Secretary of the Air Force, gave an exceptional speech on Women in Engineering.

She talked about engineering being at the root of future technology expansion.

She listed ten reasons why more women are not in engineering and ten reasons why they should be, about the increasing number of women students in engineering schools, and about the fact that many engineers treat their female colleagues as invisible.

She told a story about a time early in her career when, *even though she was giving a lecture, one student assumed she was a secretary!*

All that sounded familiar, but the true story has still to be told.

Then I thought about my own career in engineering and my experiences and I decided to share with you "The True Story."

Whatever faults the Communist regime had, it had two good qualities: women were equal with men, and college tuition was free. Admission was based solely on merit and doing well on admission tests.

I finished the Hydrotechnical Construction Faculty in Bucharest at the top of my class, with a Master of Science in Civil Engineering.

After working a few years in Romania, I defected to the United States via Greece.

My first employment in America was with the Florida Department of Environmental Protection as a stormwater engineer. I had to review construction plans for compliance with Florida's regulations, and issue permits. First, I had to learn and understand Florida's rules and regulations. What a job that was! I remember having my big academic dictionary next to me and looking up words that I did not know.

Less than two years after my arrival in America, I passed the examination to be a licensed professional engineer in Florida.

After working for the state, it was time to move on. A company owner approached me with an offer to join his firm, with the promise of becoming a partner later on. So, I worked myself to death for a small salary to build up the company that I'd have part-ownership in someday.

When I went to the University of Florida to enroll in a Ph.D. program in Hydraulics, Professor Christianson asked me to move to the campus in Gainesville.

My answer was that I was the only engineer in a small company that would suffer without my help. (Also, I had concerns about my own family moving to the United States, so I needed to keep my income.)

Then the professor told me something I'll never forget: "This company you're working for is going to squeeze you like a lemon and toss you. If you were with a larger company, maybe things would be different, as they would already have made their money. No need to sacrifice your future for someone else's interest!"

Boy, that proved to be the truth. When the company grew enough to support more employees, the owner hired a seasoned engineer and offered him the vice-presidency.

When I spoke with my employer, I was told, "I never considered you as a serious candidate for partnership." Well, that was news to me!

I moved on to another company and grew as a project engineer and project manager.

Then I started my employment with the city of Jacksonville. In the beginning things were fine, because I love to work and I threw myself into it.

Then it seemed that somewhere I'd made a wrong move, or said something that offended someone in management. I found myself on someone's black list.

From there on, regardless of how much work I put into my job, regardless of my experience and input, my job was a dead end. Six times, I was passed over for promotion in favor of colleagues without my qualifications and experience.

When I challenged the unfair treatment, I was told that maybe my English was not good enough for a management position. So, I went and took classes in English grammar and business writing and novel writing, and ended up publishing two books and a series of poems.

Then, they told me that my speech was not good enough so I joined the Toastmasters and got my CTM certificate.

Now, I thought, *I have completed every requirement, and I'm at the top of the eligibility list. Now it's my turn to be promoted.* Did I get the promotion? Nope. A young man with almost no experience or qualifications got it!

I had high hopes when the new mayor was elected, and he talked about tapping into existing talent to bring the city forward. Did my employment situation change? No way! Since 1996, I have been passed over for promotion six times, regardless of my qualifications or my job accomplishments and contributions. Every time, a young man got the promotion.

And how did I know that something was cooking in the city's management and that once again I'd be passed over for promotion?

Headhunters started calling to offer me outside jobs. My answer was always the same: "I work for the city; I'm not in the market for a job."

The last headhunter answered that with scorn. "Oh, well, and how is the city treating you?"

And that's the true story.

Do It Yourself

It all started when my family joined me here in the United States back in 1986.

I had bought a starter house in Mandarin, part of Jacksonville, to shelter my family when they would arrive. To keep up with the American tradition, I furnished my kitchen with all the gadgets that I could find at K-Mart.

The house was new, but after five years certain things started to break.

Now, Mother had the old-country philosophy: when something breaks, you repair it. She did not know the American way: when something breaks you throw it away and buy a new and better one (even though it might push your credit to the limit).

So, when my K-Mart vacuum cleaner broke, my sister and I went to have it repaired. After a lot of driving around we found a small repair shop.

The owner, a ruddy, jovial, all-American man, looked at it, took a long wire like a crochet hook from the back of his shop, and shook lose some dirt from the hose. "Now, here you are! All done! Works like brand new!"

Amazed and utterly relieved I asked, "And how much do I owe you?"

"Well, nothing! It's the Fourth of July weekend, enjoy it!"

On the drive back home, my sister and I could not get over how nice and how good-looking the man was: "That's truly the American way," I was boasted to my sister, who was newly arrived in America.

Well, when we got home and finished boasting to mother about our good fortune, we resumed the cleaning and we noticed that our brand-new brush had been replaced with a brush so used that it was not usable any longer.

So that was the price we paid for a little bit of dirt loosening!

Since then, little by little, I have learned to do things myself.

Next time the vacuum cleaner broke I bought a belt from K-Mart and, following the instructions on the belt bag, I replaced it myself.

Now, ten years later, living in a better home in San Marco, I had a better Sears vacuum cleaner that broke. No big deal, I thought. I knew how to replace belts; I'd done it before.

Legs crossed on the carpet, reading glasses perched on the tip of my nose, rivulets of sweat falling from my hairline, I tried to pry open the vacuum cleaner. No way; it was built like a bomb! There was no way to open it! I remembered that the previous one I'd fixed had had a rotor, and the belt went around it, but this one did not even open! Sweaty, swearing, I was thinking, *I'm over the hill, no wonder! Not to mention my eyesight!* It is a good thing that my neighbors do not know Romanian. Otherwise, they would have had a hard time associating the high-heeled woman, dressed like a peacock, leaving the house wearing French perfume, with the woman who was swearing like a buggy driver--that's the Romanian equivalent to, "swearing like a sailor"!

I persisted in poking around the vacuum cleaner, and after a while, a little knob up front moved, and the carcass opened. "So there!" I exclaimed triumphantly. "I knew I could do it!"

Have you noticed that all things break on the weekend?

Now the San Marco house was beautiful, home but it had old plumbing!

One Friday afternoon, coming home exhausted from the office and looking forward to the relaxing weekend, I noticed that the kitchen sink drain was stopped.

I called Turner Plumbing, just around the corner on Hendricks.

"Currently our office is closed. Our working hours are from 8:00 a.m. to 5:00 p.m. Please leave a message."

"I need a plumber first thing tomorrow morning, please!"

The next day, Saturday, I start calling at 7:00 a.m. I figured that if the plumber came by my home first thing in the morning, I'd still have time to do the grocery shopping and cleaning.

At 9:00 a.m. the office manager responded. "Turner Plumbing!"

"I need a plumber right away!"

"Well, today is Saturday! Our hourly rate is $40 an hour, but today is overtime, so we charge $60.00 an hour!"

"That's fine--please send him immediately!"

How much time would the plumber need to open a sink drain? *Half an hour at most,* I reassured myself.

At 1:00 p.m., after lunch, two men arrived.

"I asked for one plumber, why are two men showing up?" Numbers and dollar signs were multiplying in my head.

"The other one is my helper! You know, if I need something he'll bring it to me!" said one man.

I showed them the sink.

An hour later the worker asked me, "Can we move the dishwasher?"

"What's wrong with the dishwater?" I asked.

"Well, the plumbing from the sink goes behind the dishwasher."

"O.K. but hurry up. I still have a lot of things I need to do today!"

Two hours later, the dishwasher on one side, all pipes cut, the man asked: "Do you have a place where we can reach the pipe from underneath the house?"

"Yes, please go in the half basement, someone can crawl beneath. Send the helper!" I said.

"Oh no! I can't go there! What if there are spiders or mice?" the helper complained.

"O.K.," the worker said, "I'll go."

Meanwhile the helper, a blonde, heavy guy, with hair down to his shoulders, looked my sister and me over. "Do you guys have any Vodka?

"What?"

"You are Russians, aren't you?"

"What?"

"Yeah, I really like the Stolichnaya. Do you have any Stoli?"

I took my eyes off my wristwatch and looked him over. The guy was hung over, maybe on drugs. I started to fear that they would leave with the job not done.

"Don't worry," the helper said in a slurred voice. "The tee's clogged. He'll cut the tee and be done!"

"What? How long does it take? Do you have what you need in the truck to replace it?"

"Well, if we don't, you can go and get it."

"And who pays for your time while I'm gone?"

"You of course, we work for you!"

Well, to make a long story short, five hours and four hundred dollars later, they were ready to leave, and I was left to clean up after them.

Since then, I've learned that pouring a little Clorox down the drains from time to time keeps the drain open and prevent clogging.

I also learned some more do-it-yourself tricks, but I'll tell you about them in my next story!

Dealing with Computers

JACKSONVILLE, FLORIDA 2001

About two years ago, my sister and I decided that we really needed a computer at home. After all, how far can anyone go in life without "The Internet: Connection to the World?"

So, we went to Sam's to shop for a computer. Now, I wanted to stick with what I knew, a solid HP computer, but my sister wanted the most updated and sophisticated system on the market at that time: a Sony computer with a flat monitor, speaker boxes, Microsoft XP operating system, etc.

And what was the computer advertised for? Home movie production!

Now we are engineers, my sister, my brother, and I. What would we do with the capability to produce home movies?

But, you don't know my sister; if she sets her mind on something, it's going to happen. I even threw in a fancy new computer desk to go with the fancy new computer.

One concession that I succeeded in negotiating with my sister was to put the new desk and computer in my room, since we had no spare room for it. That way, at least, I could check my e-mail and maybe follow my inspiration any time the muse paid me a visit.

We brought the boxes home (including the desk, which also came in a neat box), and we stacked them in my room. That was the extent of the help I got from my family. The boxes were now in my room; I had to take care of them.

How? Nobody cared! It was my responsibility now!

Have you ever put together a computer? It has an instruction manual; actually, every part of it has a sketch and an instruction book. I can assure you: you need a Ph.D. to decipher the sketches. Buried in cables and connections, nuts and bolts, I had to figure it out. Otherwise, I wouldn't have a bed to sleep in, because until I put the desk together, everything was laid out on top of my bed.

What about the Internet connection: should I choose AOL, DLS, or Comcast?

Well, I first tried a dial-up connection with AOL (America OnLine) because the software came free with the computer. The connection was impossible. The computer had to dial a phone number, and I was lucky if I got the connection for a few minutes before a prompt on the screen was telling me, "Sorry you lost the connection!" or "This site is not permitted!" And who established which sites I was not permitted to watch?

Then, I tried DSL. I had constant problems, and it was a year before I found out the truth from a BellSouth repairman: that my house's internal telephone wiring was so old that it could not support the DSL connection. Finally, I switched to Comcast, and everything fell into place. A guy actually came to the house at the time he said he would come, drilled a hole in my wall, and installed the internet cable. It was simple!

Then, I could start calling Sony Support and Microsoft Support to install my software.

Since I had done so well with my computer installation, my confidence in my abilities skyrocketed, and I tried to install an engineering program that I wanted to work with. But it turned out that this software was not compatible with my computer operating system XP, but with the older version, Windows 98.

No big deal, I told myself. I would just install Windows 98 on my computer. Guess what? The entire system crashed! I lost everything I had on my computer!

It took hours on the phone with Sony tech support to reinstall the operating system and everything else.

Now, that was my experience as a customer dealing with the computer giants. How about the computer specialists dealing with customers like me? Here is a supposedly true story as related by a survivor of telephone support work (I found this one on the Internet):

I used to work in a computer store and one day we had a gentleman phone in with a smoking power supply. The service rep was having a bit of trouble convincing this guy that he had a hardware problem.

Service rep:Sir, something has burned within your power supply.

Customer:I bet that there is some command that I can put into the AUTOEXEC.BAT that will take care of this.

Service rep:There is nothing that software can do to help you with this problem.

Customer:I know that there is something that I can put in, some command... Maybe it should go into the CONFIG.SYS.

[After a few minutes of going round and round]

Service rep:Okay, I am not supposed to tell anyone this but there is a hidden command in some versions of DOS that you can use. I want you to edit your AUTOEXEC.BAT and add the last line as C:DOSNOSMOKE and reboot your computer.

[Customer does this]

Customer: It is still smoking.

Service rep: I guess you'll need to call Microsoft and ask them for a patch for the NOSMOKE.EXE.

[The customer then hung up. We thought that we had heard the last of this guy but NO... he calls back four hours later]

Service rep:Hello Sir, how is your computer?

Customer:I called Microsoft and they said that my power supply is incompatible with their NOSMOKE.EXE and that I need to get a new one. I was wondering where I can get it done and how much it will cost...

The Cat

I'M A CITY GIRL!

At least that's my excuse for knowing nothing about country living, including gardening and domestic animal care.

Not even a pet!

I know it's disgusting, but that's how I was until we bought the house in Jacksonville, Florida; an old Victorian home, red brick with white columns at the entrance porch and a large back yard.

Then, I had to learn something about gardening, as I had to keep up with the neighborhood. I learned to plant flowers and take care of them, to water and cut the grass, and rake the leaves.

We learned, my sister Mady and I, how to plant citrus trees beneath the canopy of the majestic oak trees already in the back yard.

We arranged white patio tables and chairs, the old fashioned kind that looked like white lace, in the back yard. We inherited with the house a fine outdoor fire place, or barbeque pit, built of concrete blocks with an iron grate in top of it. We never used the fire place, though.

Now, all my neighbors have cats and dogs; I don't have a pet and do not desire one. Too much work to clean after them!

Nevertheless, cats roam the neighborhood and end up lounging in my shaded back yard.

The other day Mady, my sister, was telling me:

"Go and look on the back of the oak tree, next to the fence. What is that?'

I looked and saw a cat squeezed into a small place at the base of the tree between the fence and the trunk. I probably looked more afraid than the cat, and the cat didn't move. Judging by her small head it was a young cat, spotted white with black.

"Maybe she is sick," I thought, and "maybe she will die and what then? What Am I going to do with a dead cat?"

"Well, nature has its course, I don't need to interfere," I reassured myself and quietly crept away from the tree.

The first thing the next morning, I went to check on the cat. She was still there squeezed between the tree trunk and the fence, but she was not dead. She didn't move, and looked at me with calm, all knowing eyes.

Again, I thought, "Nature has its course. It's not for me to interfere."

But inside, I was worried. "Why she has not moved? Is she going to die?"

The following morning, when I approached the place, the cat sprang out. I looked and saw four little kittens on the ground, all very small, the size of half of my palm. They were spotted like their mother, white with black and one entirely black, all alive. They were moving, raising their small heads and looking at me, trying the strength of their legs, crawling one on top of the other.

Now everything was clear to me. The cat had been giving birth to her four cubs.

The following day, watching from my observation point in my chair, I saw the cat taking the cubs, one by one, each in her mouth by the skin of their necks, and transporting them to a more spacious and secure place.

And what was the place? The enclosed barbeque pit, covered with the iron grate.

I swear, I had nothing to do with it! It was her decision and her action alone!

I could not believe how smart she was: she was looking for a safe place for her kittens, where the big birds could not see them and snatch them. First she tried the groove at the base of the tree, squeezed next to the fence, and then the fire pit. She had it all planned in her head!

Who said the animals do not think, or have feelings, or have strong maternal instincts. She proved to be smarter than me and more courageous, for sure!

The Cat (Part 2)

In the mornings, my sister Mady and I split our tasks split between us. I take care of the front yard and Mady takes care of the back yard.

In the front yard, on one side of the house, we have a magnificent magnolia tree that hovers over the two story house. I bought the house (twenty some years ago) enchanted with the magnolia tree when it was in full bloom.

One of my chores is to rake the magnolia tree leaves, almost on a daily basis. Besides raking the leaves, I have to weed and water the flower beds. It takes about one full hour every morning. After I'm done, I like to say: "Time well spent!"

When I finished my work and went back in the back yard, Mady told me: "I saw the Cat carrying one of her kittens, the black one, from the fire pit toward the side fence, toward the next-door neighbor.

"Let me look." So, I went to look. Inside the fire pit I could only find three kittens left instead of four.

"So Mady was right, the cat had transported her kittens again." As I looked down in the fire pit, straining my neck to see, I noticed the kittens were swarming, one on top of the other, moving like they were dreaming, for their eyes were closed. (I was told that children when born have their eyes closed, too.)

When I turned around, I noticed that the cat was sitting behind me, at some distance, calmly watching my every move, as she was firmly standing her ground. Was she afraid that I'd harm her kittens?

I went back to sit on the chair and after a while, I noticed the cat carrying her kittens, one after the other, toward the next door property.

Now, we have the back yard totally fenced in, as the back yard is our oases, our little Paradise. But the cats dig beneath the wooden fence so they can travel from one property to the other.

(Just a thought: when traveling along Interstates look at the solid retaining walls on each side--the noise, or sound barriers--that protect the nearby houses from the noise of the Interstate and notice on the lower part of these walls there are small round holes for the animals to cross from one side to the other. We have the same thing in my fence, only the holes were dug by the animals.)

Now, my next-door neighbor is a country girl! She (unlike me) knows how to care for domestic animals! (I'm using the term "girl" loosely as obviously both my neighbor and I are well over a girl's age.)

Like I said, the front yard of my neighbor is what one can call a "Disney Land" for cats!

For the kittens, she put up a plastic storage bin (like the blue ones that you buy from Wal-Mart) turned upside down with a small doorway cut into. Then, she installed a bottle with a drip line, so the kittens would have fresh water, and put bowls of cat food inside. A blanket covers the kittens' house when the nights are cold. Her entire front yard is covered with red cypress mulch like a big litter box for the cats. Colored kites hang from the skeleton trees and bright colored plastic birds and flowers hang form the bushes. I saw cats playing and jumping to catch the plastic birds and flowing kites.

I really don't care for what it does to the neighborhood's aesthetics, but it is indeed a "Disney Land" for cats.

No wonder my cat moved her kittens on my neighbor's yard.

I, for ones, do not blame her!

Spiritual Growth

I think that I'm selling myself to readers through my writing, or selling my ideas and my beliefs, and through my projects as an engineer, I'm selling my knowledge, experience, and talent to the public.

But now I have nothing to sell! My brain is flat dead as a pancake!

Nothing!

Have you heard of writer's block?

I don't from where inspiration comes. Before, when I had something to write about, my thoughts were right there, in the front of my brain, already organized. All I had to do was type them and print them. I wrote feverishly, like a convulsion, it was something I *had to do*!

(By the way, to this day, even after I have published six books, my sister Mady is not convinced that I personally wrote these books; she thinks I paid somebody else to write them, and she points out my spelling mistakes every time, as proof that I cannot write!)

But now, nothing, my brain is placid, no activity, no waves!

Do you believe in inspiration by muses and divine forces? Where are they now?

I read somewhere about two illustrious writers, Dostoyevsky and Hemingway--two of my favorite writers--who made public comments to the effect that writing came to them as if dictated by outside spirits.

I also read that when Hemingway thought the inspiration was gone, he committed suicide, so important had the writing become for him; it had taken over his life.

There are courses you can take on how to overcome writer's block: in these courses, they say that you have to take it easy and go with the flow just to keep your mind's and soul's doors open. The theory goes that at the right time something will come across your path and inspire your next writing.

✱✱✱

Have you ever tried to reconnect with friends from high school? Here in the United States it's pretty easy with all the different web sites that invite you to reconnect with your past and to find former high school buddies.

I attended high school back in Bucharest Romania. God only knows how many years ago that was!

This year, while searching the internet, I found a high school picture that had my name on it!

A former schoolmate of mine, now established in Germany, had posted pictures about our school, Sava, in Bucharest.

I contacted him via e-mail and found about some of our other school friends.

One day at work, a message flashed across my computer board: "Flash from the Past!" with two pictures attached: 7th grades classmates from back in Romania. I stared transfixed at the pictures and recognized my face, young, smiling, unmarred by the world's harshness. "Do you remember me?" the e-mailer asked. "I'm Willie, the tall guy standing in the back row next to the teacher."

As a matter of fact, I did not remember Willie at all; I don't remember talking to him even once while I was in school.

It turned out that Willie was established in Ashville, Tennessee. He had a similar story to mine: He emigrated from Romania, first to Canada, then to the United States. His life story was similar to mine in that he had also become an engineer. He was actually the Technical Director of an aerospace company in Ashville. Quite impressive!

You never know when someone new--or old in this case-- will cross your path, touch your soul, and push you to the next level of spiritual growth and awareness.

Willie did this for me. He had read one of my books, *Athens* and that's how he found me on the internet, through Google.

Willie suggested that I read a few books by Taylor Caldwell. He thought that I would benefit as a writer by reading Ms. Caldwell's books.

I have to admit that I hadn't heard of Taylor Caldwell before. And what a pity that was, because I found out from Wikipedia that she was one of the most recognizable and prolific Anglo-American Writers.

I followed Willie's advice and borrowed a book called *Great Lion of God* from the library. The book depicts the life of Paul of Tarsus. Then I read *Dear and Glorious Physician*, about the Apostle Luke.

What a wealth of information and spiritual enrichment I discovered by reading these books.

****

I don't know if I'll write another book in my life, but this time of calmness I have now is for my spiritual growth, for my soul's enrichment, and for me to step to the next level of self-awareness. And when the time is right, I'll share it with my readers.

Snippets.

always thought of myself as a person who likes to help others, and therefore I always got a good night sleep, my conscience clear that I was on the right path toward enlightenment, until...

It was midday and mid-summer in Florida, hot, very hot...

I barely made it to body pump class at the gym. For those who are not familiar with the class, it means working out with weights.

I had my head down, not paying attention to anything beyond the task at hand, trying to get my equipment in line before the class started.

It's common practice at the gym--everybody minds their own business and nobody talks to anybody else. They all look intently at their phones before the class starts, and rush out the door when the class finishes.

I heard a small voice next to me: "How long have you been doing this?"

Without glancing up, I responded: "For years"

The question came back once more: "For how long?"

This time I looked up and saw a small woman in her fifties, maybe more, definitely not an athlete, struggling to get her equipment.

I responded again: "for years" and continued with my work, without giving it another thought.

Then, a man situated just behind me, intervened.

I knew the man, for he'd been attending the same class for a while, and in my opinion, he was a bore. He was always asked the instructor about his aches and pains and even about his diet.

As he was starting to aid the small woman with her equipment, he said "It doesn't matter if you are the queen on the dance class, here you are nothing!"

He proceeded to instruct the woman how to use the equipment and to start with small weights and progress gradually.

And I thought, "Maybe he knows the woman and she is indeed a dancer, even though she does not look the part! But it was nice of him to help her and give her good advice!"

I watched the woman throughout the class, as she was seated in front on me, and noticed that she was struggling, but did not give up. She finished the class.

I went home, but somehow the matter did not sit right with me.

I couldn't stop thinking about it.

And then, I realized the truth: the man behind me was shaming me in front of the class for not helping the woman, and I did not even realize.

I was the only one there who had gone to the dance classes!

He was talking about me and the fact that I had turned my back on the woman who was asking for my help!

It was a minor incident, but it helped me realize how other people saw me, and I was not the person I thought I was, a person willing to help…

I'd become like everybody else, rushing in and out of the classes, checking my phone and not even looking around me, engrossed in my own persona and my own thoughts.

Confessions

There are certain traits of character you are born with.

Do parents, school, or society have anything to do with who you are?

Of course: they can help polish some of your traits, tame the undesirable ones, and improve on your good qualities when everything is working well.

But does it really change who you are?

I don't think so!

I was born with a lot of ambition, pride, and courage, even though on the outside I was a little gray mouse, hardly ever voicing my opinion, hardly asking for anything at all. I had my world inside me and kept my own company.

I think I had an inherited trait from my mother's side of the family, and her Macedonian heritage.

The Macedonian people, more so than the Greek people, are very proud and ambitious. They're proud of their heritage (they are the direct descendants of Alexander the Great) and are fearless people, the conquerors of the entire world. Being the best, achieving the most, and flaunting your wealth and successes among your peers and relatives are trademarks of Macedonian people.

So, as a student, I was always the first in my class.

I spent so much time on my studies and made so many sacrifices at the expense of fun time and play to become the best. If I failed, it affected my morale and wellbeing!

I worked alone, in silence. All the smart kids at the school were my competitors. It was like a running race.

But life has its own hard lessons to teach.

No matter how hard I have worked, in the end I have not achieved much of anything in my private or professional life.

And the reason is that I worked alone!

No one can conquer the world alone!

And there are lessons that I hoped to have learned!

My profession is as an engineer.

Even though I excelled at my trade, I did not get the recognition for it materially or otherwise.

I noticed that my male colleagues were working together as a team, never backstabbing anyone, having fun from time to time, working and playing sports together, telling their innermost secrets to one another, and not betraying their friends.

Meanwhile, I was alone, working by myself, and being sabotaged and passed over by my men colleagues.

When I was put in a position of responsibility, I did not have a team of people I could count on to do the work.

No matter how fair I was to them, they did not support me. I was alone, and no matter how hard I worked, I could not do everything by myself.

So, I failed! And now, after years, I was reminded by my behavior by my partner.

He plays in a band, and I suggested he plays solo for indeed, he is very good.

But he answered that he preferred to play with his bandmates for each of them are doing their best, and it is so much more fun!

So, he preferred his team over glory for himself!

What a marvelous lesson he taught me!

For indeed he is very successful and nobody takes away his fame--they all enhance his glory, and let him shine, even though he stays in the background!

Dreams

This morning was the funeral of my cousin's husband, Nelu, in Focsani, Romania.

And I had a dream last night.

It is said that while you are sleeping deeply your spirit and your astral being can leave your body and travel in time and space.

Whether true or not, I don't know, but I frequently dream in color of places I've never been before, or even seen on TV or read about.

Maybe, I'm remembering places where I lived or traveled to in past lives?

I don't know.

You have to know that Focsani is the natal place of my father, and his father's father, a place in the part of Romania called Moldova, where traditions and customs are kept unchanged over generations, where vampires and witches live, an enchanted place where the best wines are made.

So, last night, I dreamed that I rescued a little girl, from a barrel and went inside a house to wash her hands.

Inside the room was a bad woman, a bad witch, if you want to call her that, and she had two magnificent sphinxes that she kept tied up.

I looked up at the sphinxes and ordered them to move and wait for me outside. And they did; they freed themselves and went outside to wait for me, as if I had magical powers and could transmit my thoughts without speaking out loud.

A strange dream, I thought. I could not fathom its meaning.

Then, I talked to my cousin and asked about the funeral.

She told me that she'd buried her husband that morning, but before she could do that, she had to unearth her mother, Olga, and her aunt, Maria, to make space for them because cemetery space in Romania is very limited. An Orthodox Priest (that's the predominant religion in Romania) prayed for them as well.

Now, my dream made sense to me.

It was an old story in my father's family that one of his sisters, Maria, was forcefully married when she was only 16 years old to a rich old man, and she suffered a lot. She placed a curse on all women of the family to suffer in love.

And today the curse was broken as her soul was freed.

The two magnificent sphinxes were my two aunts, Olga and Maria.

You have to know that all members of my father's family were magnificent, beautiful creatures, with Italian and Armenian heritage.

True, or not, or just my wishful thinking, I don't know.

I'm just telling stories.

Rea-Silvia Costin @2024

Saint Phothios Chapel

Good Friday morning.

I drive to Saint Augustine almost every Friday. It's about an hour from Jacksonville, where I live. I take the A1A south route along the Atlantic Ocean coast, because the views are out of this world: palm trees and luxurious vegetation, beautiful houses, and big mansions built right on the beaches.

As I drive along the narrow, two-way roads, from time to time I can glimpse the ocean waters. They're sometimes furious with big waves crashing on the shores and at other times calm and smooth like oil.

I like to go on Fridays to avoid the weekend crowds of visitors, for St. Augustine is the oldest town in America where the Spaniards first descended. It's full of old buildings and narrow streets, an enchanting little town where time has stood still for centuries.

On George Street, the main historic route, stands the Saint Phothios Capel, a small Greek Orthodox Church.

As the story goes, when they were digging for some construction project, the workers found a cross and the chapel was built on that location. It is an enchanted little place with an inside garden adorned with blue flowers and white benches, and inside the chapel the walls are skillfully painted and adorned with icons of Crist and other saints and angels.

As you approach the altar there are two marble boxes full of sand where candles are lighted; one on the left side facing the icon of Virgin Mary with the baby Jesus is for the wishes of the living souls. On the right side, the one for the souls of the departed is watched over by the icon of St. Zacharias.

Old and precious icons and artifacts adorn the walls of the other two little chambers.

I go there every Friday morning to light candles for myself on the left side, and for my dear departed ones on the right side.

Phothos means light, and it's the place where I go to feel closer to God. Hardly anyone goes there on Friday mornings. I can pray in peace and light my candles.

So, on Good Friday I went to light candles. As the Christ is raised from the dead on Holy Saturday at midnight, so the dead are risen from the graves and ascend to Heaven with Christ, or so the Bible says.

After I finished, I went to sit on the bench in the interior church's garden. It was so peaceful!

Then I heard a scream, a beastly scream coming from behind the church's thick walls and my heart stopped. For I recognized the devil's roaring trying to get as many souls as it could.

Think what you may, but I know that the battles have gone on for centuries between invisible forces of good and bad, between right and wrong, between God and Devil, between good people and evil people.

REA-SILVIA COSTIN, P.E. @ 2024

The Picture

About two years ago I posted my profile on Facebook. I chose my best picture, nothing erotic; I don't go for such a thing, as I consider myself a classy lady.

I followed closely my celebrity crush (a man of course) on Facebook.

After a while a picture of that celebrity was posted on Facebook; the celebrity was holding up a letter, a love letter I might add, addressed to me (or so I thought, as my name was spelled out on the piece of paper).

To make a long story short, I ended up corresponding with said celebrity!

How, I don't know exactly.

Two years later, I showed him the picture that started it all out, and added a title to it: "Love without Limits", or "L'Amour sans chains"

"This picture of you hooked me up", I said.

"Who sent you this picture?" you replied angrily.

"You, of course, who else?" I replied, a little confused.

"How many times have I told you I'm not on any social media!" you replied.

"But it is your picture, isn't it? And my name is spelled out on the letter you're holding, isn't?" I replied even more confused, for I'd kept that picture close to my heart for two years.

"How can I send you a picture on Facebook when I'm not even on Facebook? Don't you see that the picture is edited?" you replied angrily.

Now, I started to look closely at my precious picture with the magnifying glass.

To my surprise, I saw that he was holding a puppy in his lap, and someone attached, or superimposed the letter in front.

"Yeah, it is fake, I can see it now. That's why you looked so happy in it, for you were holding the puppy in your arms," I replied totally deflated.

"Well, I still wished that the picture was real and you'd sent the love letter to me," I added.

"Somebody did you a favor, for I fell in love with you."

I'm a hopeless romantic!

Diana

My father was born in a small town in North Eastern Romania called Focsani. The entire region north east of the Carpathian Mountains is called Moldova and it's famous for its vineyards. As the men of the Costin family went to schools and universities, built their families, and moved out of Focsani, the women, Olga and Maria, remained in the patriarchal town.

Fast forward a few generations. My nephew, Andi, (we call him Bobita, for his handful of black, curly, hair and black eyes), inherited from his father a country place in a village called Urechesti, several kilometers outside Focsani.

I went to visit Urechesti in 2001 on my trip to Romania and I remember it as an enchanted place.

From the main route you enter the country estate along a hill covered in vines with glossy grapes hanging heavy.

On one side were the old patriarchal houses, a row of small houses where the grandparents lived; on another side were the new houses freshly painted blue for the new generations. A few steps lead to the new house.

In the middle of the yard was a well, and then a patch of vineyards on the other side.

My brother-in-law used to make wine every year and gracefully gave it to the entire family.

Now the place belongs to Bobita.

And Bobita's great love is horses. Therefore, as the new Master, he went ahead and bought himself a horse, but not just any horse. His horse is a three year old mare called Diana, and as her name suggests, she behaves like a princess.

My nephew who lives in town, in Focsani, has to go every day to Urechesti to bring fresh water and food to his beloved mare, to clean up the stall, to polish his mare, and treat her with apples and carrots.

Now, when Diana is left alone she finds it right to eat an entire row of grapes, even when they were only buds. She plays with the dogs and waits for her beloved Master to take good care of her.

And Bobita comes dutifully every day, skipping lunch, to take care of Diana, and he developed gastritis.

What love makes you do!

But wait! Loves goes both ways!

The other day, Bobita felt sick and went to lie down in his bedroom at the back of the new house and dozed off.

A soft massage rubbed his aching belly, and he woke up to find Diana rubbing his stomach with her nostrils.

How had that happened? There are the front stairs leading to the house, then three rooms with their own doorways before reaching his bedroom.

How did the mare know to find him, or that his stomach was hurting?

Love works miracles!

Now the logistics came in place as the rooms were too small for the mare to turn around and Bobita directed Diana's every step backwards and out of the house.

And Love grows...